from the Hidden

An investigation of the four horsemen

Theresa Garcia

Copyright © 2004 by Theresa Garcia

From The Hidden
by Theresa Garcia

Printed in the United States of America

ISBN 1-591608-02-3

All rights reserved solely by the author. The author guarantees all contents are original and do not infringe upon the legal rights of any other person or work. No part of this book may be reproduced in any form without the permission of the author. The views expressed in this book are not necessarily those of the publisher.

Unless otherwise indicated, Bible quotations are taken from the New King James Version of the Bible. Copyright © 1995 by Thomas Nelson, Inc.

Scripture quotations marked by (OKJ) are taken from the Old King James Version of the Bible.

Cover design by Keith and Donna Cherry
(waymaker@sbcglobal.net)

Cover Copyright © 2004 by Theresa Garcia

Dedication

To my husband, Cass, who God chose for me
before the foundation of the world.

Acknowledgments

I gratefully acknowledge the following persons who helped in some way with my book, From the Hidden.

Firstly, thanks to my greatest friends now and forever, I love you dearly and appreciate you most, my husband, children and children-in-law. Blessings and gratitude to Carolyn Reinneck and the Monday morning prayer group, and Bonnie Wallace and the Tuesday morning prayer group who coined the phrase, "a copy on every coffee table." God bless Myrtle Beardsley for being there to encourage me. To Deane and Gwen Reeser who taught me to love Israel, also to Gwen for her skills in the editing of the book, many thanks. To Katy Murray and Evelyn Kinsella for encouraging me in my teaching gift and Nina de Gala, who facilitated my ministry in Iowa, I am forever grateful. I wish to give special thanks to Dave and Joyce Meyer who encouraged me when I needed it the most. May God's favor rest on Keith and Donna Cherry, whose expertise in marketing, research, typing, technical advice and input on all things artistic made this book possible. May any blessing that proceeds from this book accrue to their account.

Finally, and most significantly, to my constant companion and Best Friend, the Holy Spirit of God, who brought this work to fruition. I covet His continual blessing on this and future projects.

Table of Contents

Prologue xi

    Chapter 1: God's Divine Week 13

    Chapter 2: The Judgment of the Nations 21

    Chapter 3: The Antichrist Persona..31

    Chapter 4: The Four Horsemen Defined..............................41

    Chapter 5: A Dappled/Green Horse......................................51

    Chapter 6: World Conflict/World Harvest 55

    Chapter 7: The Four Horsemen Explained 67

Epilogue..81

A Word From The Author 85

Prologue

In 95 A.D., banished to the island of Patmos because he would not die, John, the beloved apostle, was given a panoramic view of things to come. Jesus' revelations to John are called, in Greek, "apo" (**from**) "kalupsis" (**the hidden**). Thus we refer to the final book in the Bible as the apocalypse.

God has many mysteries. The *"mystery of the ages, Christ in you, the hope of glory,"* (Colossians 1:27) had been revealed through the apostle Paul a generation earlier. The *"mystery of iniquity"* (2Thessalonians 2:7) still flourishes in the earth today. The *"mystery of God"* will be completed during the seven year period of the tribulation, according to Revelation 10:7.

One of the most enduring questions Bible students have desired to understand throughout the ages is this: Who are those four horsemen of the Apocalypse? They parade across history in Revelation Chapter 6. Many theories as to their identity have been suggested. We will examine them in this book in light of these words of Jesus not often considered in reference to the horsemen: *"It is also written in your law that the testimony of two men is true."* John 8:17

This rule of Bible interpretation, using the testimony of two or three witnesses, is derived from the Book of Deuteronomy. In the context of that book, the testimony of two or three witnesses is needed to condemn a man to death. But in the broader sense, it is a well-established and generally accepted rule of Bible interpretation. Simply stated, to be accepted as accurate, it must turn up in Biblical study at least two or three times.

And so we ask the question: Where, besides in the Book of Revelation, do we find the four horsemen? Could it be the secret of their true identity is hidden somewhere in the law or the prophets?

Before we answer those questions, let us see where our generation fits into "God's Divine Week," and how much time we have before the horsemen come charging onto the world scene.

Chapter 1

God's Divine Week

The universe is approximately 14 billion years old. This is a fact upon which scientists and the Jewish sages generally agree.[1] Somewhere in those past ages ancient animals roamed, urban populations flourished, and then a cataclysmic event occurred.

This is clearly recorded in this Biblical record, in verse 2.

> *1In the beginning God created the heavens and the earth.*
> *2The earth was **without form, and void**; and darkness was on the face of the deep. And the Spirit of God was hovering over the face of the waters.*
> *3Then God said, 'Let there be light', and there was light.*
> Genesis 1:1-3 (emphasis added).

Notice in verse 2 that darkness covered everything. God took the prophet Jeremiah backwards in time and showed him this dismal scene. Many scholars believe verse 2 refers to the destruction of a pre-Adamic civilization, which resulted from Satan's rebellion against God. Here is the way Jeremiah recorded it:

*23I beheld the earth, and indeed it was **without form, and void**; And the heavens, they had no light.*

24I beheld the mountains, and indeed they trembled, And, all the hills moved back and forth.

25I beheld, and indeed there was no man, And, all the birds of the heavens had fled.

26I beheld, and indeed the fruitful land was a wilderness, And all its cities were broken down, At the presence of the Lord, By His fierce anger.

27For thus says the Lord: 'The whole land shall be desolate; Yet I will not make a full end.

28For this shall the earth mourn, And, the heavens above be black, Because I have spoken. I have purposed and will not relent, Nor will I turn back from it."
Jeremiah 4:23-28 (emphasis added)

The blackness persisted throughout eons of ages until God's appointed time. And then, when it pleased Him, He gave the command in Genesis 1:3 *"Let there be light"* and the Light of the World came on the scene. Notice Genesis 1:14-18 records the creation of the sun, moon and stars did not occur until the fourth day. The light that came forth on the first day was the Light of the World, the Lord Jesus Christ:

1 In the beginning was the Word, and the Word was with God, and the Word was God.

2 He was in the beginning with God.

3 All things were made through Him, and without Him nothing was made that was made.

*4 In Him was life, and the life **was the light of men**.*

*5 And **the light shines in the darkness**, and the darkness did not comprehend it.*
John 1:1-5 (emphasis added)

And so, six thousand years ago God created Adam and gave him dominion and a mandate to rule. We know the story all too well. Let us summarize human history from Adam to this present day.

From Adam to Abraham 2,000 years – Age of Conscience.
From Abraham to Christ 2,000 years – Age of the Law.
From Christ to the present 2,000 years – Age of Grace.

Human history has one more age to enjoy, namely the Millennial (1,000 year) reign of Jesus Christ, before eternity begins.

We like the way Kenneth Copeland puts it: "For all practical purposes, 2,000 years have come and gone since Jesus' birth and ministry. Six thousand years since Adam was created. You and I are being squeezed between 6,000 years of time behind us and another 1,000 years ahead of us. The 1,000 years facing us is the Millennial reign of Jesus of Nazareth." [2]

And this, dear readers, is what is known as "God's Divine Week." But you may consider a week to be a span of time that covers seven days, while I am speaking here of a span of time that covers 7,000 years. A single verse of Scripture can quickly erase all confusion.

> *8But beloved, do not forget this one thing, that with the Lord one day is as a thousand years, and a thousand years as one day.*
>
> 2 Peter 3:8

One of the purposes of the seven-day creation story was to prefigure the 7,000 years of human history. God is always working toward perfection. We know that in Hebrew, seven is the number of perfection.

Furthermore, God as much as told Isaiah that the creation story told the whole story:

> *9Remember the former things of old, For I am God, and there is no other; I am God, and there is none like Me,*
> ***10Declaring the end from the beginning...***
>
> Isaiah 46:9-10 (emphasis added)

Yahweh said something very similar through King Solomon, the wisest man who ever lived:

> **9That which has been is what will be**, That which is done is what will be done, And there is nothing new under the sun.
> **10**Is there anything of which it may be said, "See, this is new?" ***It has already been in ancient times before us.***
> Ecclesiastes 1:9-10 (emphasis added)

Let us use an example to illustrate this point. The first Jewish war, recorded in Genesis 14, has Abram the Hebrew battling the kings of Babylon (Shinar) and Persia. The final Jewish war, Armageddon, has Jesus, the King of the Jews again battling, and defeating antichrist, the King of Babylon. (Jeremiah 25:26; Isaiah 14:4)

Thus we have events in the Bible playing out, all the while prefiguring future events, which God desires us to delve into and understand.

This chart illustrates what we refer to as **God's Divine Week**.

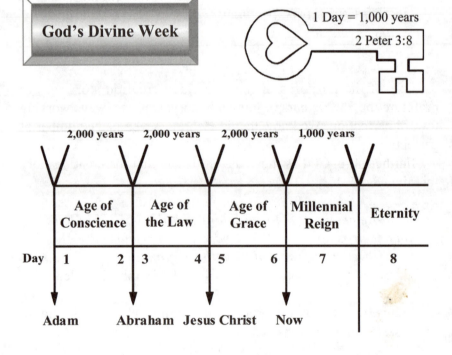

From The Hidden

Using this chart, we see a total of seven days, which we understand from 2 Peter 3:8 to be seven thousand years. Adam was created at the beginning of day one, and after the fall of man was to find God's will by using his conscience. Thus, we have the first two thousand year period called the "Age of Conscience." Unfortunately, man did not do a very good job of living by his conscience, because seventeen hundred years into human history God, who is love, sent the flood.

Love sent the flood? Yes, dear reader, for you and I would not be here today if God had not sent the flood. Mankind was deteriorating into sinfulness so rapidly that 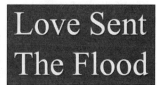 soon all men would have been hell bound. In Genesis 11, right after the flood, we see Nimrod building the Tower of Babel, again defying God. God had to do something! And so, five generations later He raised up Abraham and gave man a better way to righteousness.

The "Age of the Law" began when God cut covenant with Abraham in Genesis 15. On Mount Sinai, the Law came into fullness when Moses was given the Ten Commandments. The "Age of the Law" was fulfilled with the ministry of the Lord Jesus, who was born about 3 B.C.

The "Age of Grace" was introduced at the Last Supper:

> *26And as they were eating, Jesus took bread, blessed and broke it, and gave it to the disciples and said, "Take, eat; this is My body."*
> *27Then he took the cup, and gave thanks, and gave it to them, saying, "Drink from it, all of you.*
> *28For this is My blood of **the new covenant**, which is shed for many for the remission of sins."*
> Matthew 26:26-28 (emphasis added).

It came into fullness on Pentecost Sunday:

> *1When the Day of Pentecost had fully come, they were all with one accord in one place.*

> 2And suddenly there came a sound from heaven, as of a rushing mighty wind, and it filled the whole house where they were sitting.
> 3Then there appeared to them divided tongues, as of fire, and one sat upon each of them.
> 4And they were **all filled with the Holy Spirit** and began to speak with other tongues, as the Spirit gave them utterance.
> Acts 2:1-4 (emphasis added)

Today we are at the culmination of the "Age of Grace," also called the "Age of Faith" or the "Church Age."

We recall that when Moses came down the mountain with the Ten Commandments, he found the people in sin. As retribution, God required him to send the Levites among the people, executing **about three thousand** of them (Exodus 32:26-28). On Pentecost Sunday, the birth of the "Age of Grace," we see that **about three thousand** souls were added to the Church. (Acts 2:41) Thus we see a great truth revealed: *"The letter kills but the Spirit gives life."* (2 Corinthians 3:6)

We should be forever grateful to the Lord for allowing us to live during the "Age of Grace." In the Bible, the "Age of Grace" is also referred to as the "Last Days." The Jews always referred to days by their number, in Biblical times. Sunday was "the first day of the week," Wednesday was the "fourth day of the week," etc. God always works toward perfection, and seven is the number of perfection. Thus, the Jews were always working toward the seventh day, the Sabbath, after which they would begin again.

Reviewing our chart, we see that the last two days (or 2,000 years) before the 1,000 year Sabbath rest, are days five and six. Hence, the following scriptures refer to the "Age of Grace" as the "Last Days."

> 16But this is what was spoken by the prophet Joel:
> 17And it shall come to pass **in the last days**, says God, That I will pour out of My Spirit on all flesh...
> Acts 2:16-17 (emphasis added)

> *1But know this, that **in the last days** perilous times will come:*
> *2For men will be lovers of themselves, lovers of money, boasters, proud, blasphemers, disobedient to parents, unthankful, unholy...*
>
> 2 Timothy 3:1-2 (emphasis added)

> *17But you, beloved, remember the words which were spoken before by the apostles of our Lord Jesus Christ:*
> *18How they told you that there would be mockers in **the last time** who would walk according to their own ungodly lusts.*
>
> Jude 17-18 (emphasis added)

We are actually living at the end of the sixth, or last day. Some may ask, the last day before what? The answer is obvious; the last day before the Sabbath, or seventh day, the Millennial Age. Knowing that we are in the last day makes these words of Jesus in John so much clearer. He's telling us when the rapture will be. We are not surprised to find out we'll be raptured on the last day:

> *40And this is the will of Him who sent Me, that everyone who sees the Son and believes in Him may have everlasting life; and **I will raise him up at the last day**.*

> *44No one can come to Me unless the Father who sent Me draws him; and **I will raise him at the last day**.*

> *54Whoever eats My flesh and drinks My blood has eternal life, and **I will raise him up at the last day**.*
>
> John 6:40, 44, 54 (emphasis added)

Sometimes the words "Last Days" and "End Times" are used interchangeably, but that is incorrect. The "Last Days" began, as we have illustrated, on Pentecost. The "End Times" began, in our opinion, when the Lord's parable of the fig tree (Israel) was fulfilled and Israel became a nation again, May 15, 1948.

29"...Look at the fig tree (Israel) and all the trees (nations of prophecy).

30When they are already budding (vibrant after 1900 years of dormancy), you see and know for yourselves that summer (the judgment of the nations) is now near.

31So you also, when you see these things happening (prophecy being fulfilled), know that the kingdom of God is near.

32Assuredly I say to you, this generation (alive in 1948) will by no means pass away till all these things take place."

Luke 21:29-32 (parenthesis are author's interpretation)

The "End Times" will culminate in a period often referred to as "The Judgment of the Nations." Could it be that we are already in the time period known as "The Judgment of the Nations?" If so, what does the future hold for you and me?

Chapter 2

The Judgment of the Nations

The Judgment of the Nations is a time in history when nations will finally reap what they have sown. We recall giving certain counsel to our children many times as they were growing up: "No one ever gets away with anything." So it is also with the nations. In the last analysis, all judgment on this earth will be reduced to this question, "How did you treat Israel and the Jews?" (Matthew 25:31-46).

Many Christian and Jewish scholars believe the Judgment of the Nations began on Rosh Hashanah in the year right after 1998, the Year of the Jubilee. That is, the Judgment of the Nations began on September 11, 1999.[3]

If this is accurate, it could explain why Satan chose September 11, 2001 as the date to attack the Twin Towers in New York, sort of a return salvo.

In any event, we believe we are living in that judgment time, which is characterized by:

All previously unfulfilled prophetic wars will occur. These wars include:

The Iraqi War - Jeremiah 50, 51

The leveling of Damascus - Isaiah 17
The war of Gog and Magog – Ezekiel 38, 39
Armageddon – Revelation 19:11-21 and Zechariah 12 & 14

This knowledge **should not strike terror** in the heart of the reader, just the opposite, really. We are living in the most exciting time of history, living in the greatest nation, with an unparalleled opportunity before us. We are not here by accident. God put us here at this time because He knew that by His grace we would get the job done! What job? The job of harvesting the seed sown by the sacrifice of the martyrs, the tears of the missionaries and the prayers of mothers and fathers on their knees for the past two thousand years! If we will stay faithful to our call, and most of us will, we will *"shine like the brightness of the firmament... and the stars forever and ever."* (Daniel 12:3)

Judgments will become more rapid in succession, and more severe.

> *7For nation will rise against nation, and kingdom against kingdom. And there will be famines, pestilences and earthquakes in various places.*
> Matthew 24:7

God, who is love, will use these catastrophes and judgments to draw men to Himself.

> *9b...For when Your judgments are in the earth, The inhabitants of the world will learn righteousness.*
> Isaiah 26:9b

He will increase His glory during judgment.

> *21I will set My glory among the nations; all the nations shall see My judgment which I have executed, and My hand which I have laid on them.*
> Ezekiel 39:21

The time will finally come when the sin-laden nations will be weary and the glory will be full:

> *13Behold, is it not of the Lord of hosts that the peoples labor to feed the fire, And nations weary themselves in vain?*
> *14For the earth will be filled with the knowledge of the glory of the Lord, as the waters cover the sea.*
> Habakkuk 2:13-14

Then the Bride of Christ, the Church, will be raptured, as prophesied by Hosea: (Remember that the Age of Grace lasts two thousand years, or "two days")

> *2After two days He will revive us; On the third day He will raise us up, That we may live in His sight.*
> Hosea 6:2

After the rapture, Jesus will receive us, the Bride of Christ, at the heavenly wedding feast. We see a confirmation of the timing of this wedding feast cleverly woven into the fabric of the gospel of John:

> *1On the third day, there was a wedding...*
> John 2:1

This refers to the third day (1,000 years) of church history.

As we stated above, God always desires man to repent. Notice that even during the second half of the Tribulation, God sends angels to be seen by men, with warnings not to be ignored.

> *6Then I saw another angel flying in the midst of heaven, having the everlasting gospel to preach to those who dwell on the earth—to every nation, tribe, tongue, and people—*
> *7saying with a loud voice, "Fear God and give glory to Him, for the hour of His judgment has come; and*

worship Him who made heaven and earth, the sea and springs of water..."

9Then a third angel followed them, saying with a loud voice, **"If anyone worships the beast and his image, and receives his mark on his forehead or on his hand***,*
10he himself shall also drink of the wine of the wrath of God*, which is poured out full strength into the cup of His indignation. He shall be tormented with fire and brimstone in the presence of the holy angels and in the presence of the Lamb.*
Revelation 14:6-7, 9-10 (emphasis added)

And finally, right before the battle of Armageddon, the Lord Himself, filled with love for His rebellious children, makes one last appeal:

15Behold, I am coming as a thief. Blessed is he who watches, and keeps his garments, lest he walk naked and they see his shame.
16And they gathered them together to the place called in Hebrew, Armageddon.
Revelation 16:15-16

A review of the characteristics of the time of the Judgment of the Nations reveals: all Biblical wars will be completed, judgments will be progressively harsher and more proximate, and God's hand of mercy will be extended throughout.

As on earth, a court must be assembled in heaven, with a presiding judge, before a judgment can be pronounced. The world will have its day in court, as illustrated in both the Old and New Testaments:

9I beheld till the thrones were cast down, and the Ancient of days did sit, whose garment was white as snow, and the hair of His head like the pure wool: His throne was like the fiery flame,; and His wheels as burning fire.
10A fiery stream issued and came forth from before

Him: thousand thousands ministered unto Him; and ten thousand times ten thousand stood before Him: the judgment was set, and the books were opened...
Daniel 7:9-10 (OKJ)

2Immediately I was in the Spirit; and behold, a throne set in heaven, and One sat on the throne...

4Around the throne were twenty-four thrones, and on the thrones I saw twenty-four elders sitting, clothed in white robes and they had crowns of gold on their heads...

7Then He came and took the book out of the right hand of Him who sat on the throne...

11Then I looked, and I heard the voice of many angels around the throne, the living creatures, and the elders; and the number of them was ten thousand times ten thousand, and thousands of thousands.
Revelation 4:2, 4 and Revelation 5:7, 11(OKJ)

Let us look again at the Old King James Version of Daniel 7:10b:

10b...The judgment was set, And the books were opened."

As we have already pointed out, we believe the judgment was set on September 11, 1999 (see Chapter 2 paragraph 2). In the Bible, a punctuation mark can represent an extended period of time. We believe that we are living in a time represented by the comma after the word "set." We will continue in this time frame until after the rapture of the Church. At that time, the *"books will be opened." "And the books were opened"* is discussed in greater detail in Chapter 4.

The chart on the next page gives our analysis of what we believe will transpire during the time of the Judgment of the Nations. There is no unanimity of opinion among Bible teachers on the sequence of the events. We invite the readers to search the Scripture and see what the Holy Spirit reveals to their own hearts.

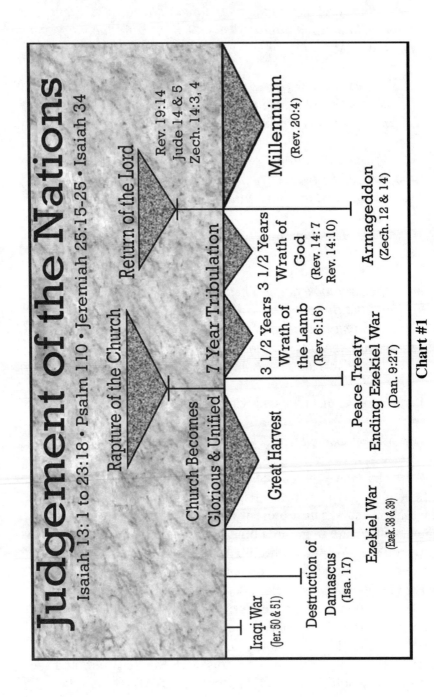

Chart #1

Some scholars believe the leveling of Damascus will be the event that triggers the war of Ezekiel 38 and 39. We agree with that view for four reasons:

1) Syria, an arch foe of Israel, does not take part in the attack against Israel in Ezekiel 38 and 39.
2) Two powerful eschatological portions of Scripture, the book of Amos and Zechariah: Chapter 9, begin with the destruction of Damascus.
3) Isaiah 17, the Chapter that prophesies "Damascus will cease from being a city," ends with three verses that appear to be the Ezekiel war. This would imply that the destruction of Damascus precedes the Ezekiel war.

> *12Woe to the multitude of many people Who make a noise like the roar of the seas, And to the rushing of nations That make a rushing like the rushing of mighty waters!*
> *13The nations will rush like the rushing of many waters; But God will rebuke them and they will flee far away, And be chased like the chaff of the mountains before the wind, Like a rolling thing before the whirlwind.*
> *14Then behold, at eventide, trouble! And before the morning, he is no more. This is the portion of those who plunder us, And the lot of those who rob us.*
> Isaiah 17:12-14

4) Building on what we have just explained, a careful reading of Jeremiah 49:23-27 seems to prophesy a naval attack by the Israelis leading to a fire in Damascus, no doubt a very powerful bomb. (Amos 1:4 confirms that fire will devour Damascus) We have emphasized verse 25. We see the prophet Jeremiah implying this in verse 25: The Syrians are attacking us. We must either destroy Damascus or evacuate Jerusalem. We choose, therefore, to destroy Damascus. (Jerusalem, of course is the city of God's joy.)

> *23Against Damascus. "Hamath and Arpad are shamed, For they have heard bad news. They are faint-*

hearted; There is trouble on the sea; It cannot be quiet.

24Damascus has grown feeble; She turns to flee. And fear has seized her. Anguish and sorrows have taken her like a woman in labor.

25Why is the city of praise not deserted, the city of My joy?

26Therefore her young men shall fall in her streets, And all the men of war shall be cut off in that day," says the Lord of hosts.

27"I will kindle a fire in the wall of Damascus, And it shall consume the palaces of Ben-Hadad."

Jeremiah 49:23-27 (emphasis added)

We will discuss the Ezekiel war in detail in Chapter 6. It is pivotal to understanding the direction to which each of the four horsemen will travel.

The first of the four horsemen, the man on the white horse, we believe will be the antichrist. As one of the most enigmatic persons in Biblical prophecy much has been written about him.

We will not name a particular person. We believe it is very insulting and presumptuous to accuse someone of being the antichrist.

Furthermore, Scripture teaches that he will be revealed **after** the rapture.

7For the mystery of lawlessness is already at work; only He who now restrains will do so until He is taken out of the way.

8And then the lawless one will be revealed, whom the Lord will consume with the breath of His mouth and destroy with the brightness of His coming.

2 Thessalonians 2:7-8

Who is "He" who restrains the antichrist, forbidding him from being revealed? He is the Body of Christ. Now we know that the Body of Christ is sometimes referred to in the feminine as the "Bride of Christ." The Body of Christ is also referred to sometimes in the masculine:

> *13till we all come to the unity of the faith and of the knowledge of the Son of God to a **perfect man**, to the measure of the stature of the fullness of Christ;*
> Ephesians 4:13 (emphasis added)

Therefore, "He" who restrains the antichrist from being revealed is none other than the "perfect man" of Ephesians 4:13. Namely, "He" is the Body of Christ.

Let us outline a series of events, which we believe will soon transpire on the earth.

1) Syria will attack Israel.
2) Israel will counterattack by sea to save Jerusalem, leveling Damascus.
3) Indignation in Russia and the Arab community will precipitate the Ezekiel War.
4) God will defeat the Russian and Arab invaders on the mountains of Israel (see Chapter 6)
5) A diplomat will come from Syria to Jerusalem to broker a seven-year peace treaty with Israel. This diplomat is the antichrist:

> *27Then he shall confirm a covenant with many for one week; But in the middle of the week he shall bring an end to sacrifice and offering. And on the wing of abominations shall be one who makes desolate, Even until the consummation, which is determined, Is poured out on the desolate.*
> Daniel 9:27

Let us read on to see what else the Scripture has to say about this diabolical man.

Chapter 3

The Antichrist Persona

Before we attempt to identify the four horsemen, we must understand where the antichrist comes from, since he rides on one of the horses. He is identified in Revelation 13:1 as a beast with seven heads. Those seven heads represent the kingdoms that have come against national Israel throughout history. (See chart below)

The vision of the four beasts in Daniel 7 identifies the four world powers that dominated ancient Jerusalem, described as beasts.

Seven kingdoms against national Israel:

Egypt	Daniel 7:4 - 8
Assyria	"Four Great Beasts"
Babylon..........................Lion	
Medo-Persia...................Bear	
Greece............................Leopard	
Rome..............................Dreadful Beast	
Revived Rome	

Chart #2

A comparison of the beasts in Daniel 7:4-8 and the description of antichrist in Revelation is striking:

> 2*Now the beast which I saw was like a **leopard**, his feet were like the feet of a **bear**, and his mouth like the mouth of a **lion**. And the dragon gave him his power, his throne, and great authority.*
>
> Revelation 13:2 (emphasis added)

We render this description to infer: Now the antichrist was like a Greek (**leopard**), his feet walked where the Medo-Persians (**bear**) walked, and his mouth devoured what the Babylonians (**lion**) devoured.

Thus we conclude that the antichrist will be of Greek origin, take over Iraq as the Medo-Persians did and subsequently "devour" Jerusalem as the Babylonians did. In fact, the antichrist is referred to as the King of Babylon (Isaiah 14:4) and the King of Sheshach (Jeremiah 25:26). Sheshach is a code name for Babylon. The antichrist is also called the Assyrian (Isaiah 10:24 and 14:25 and Micah 5:5,6). Let us examine our theory in light of that name and see if our model holds up.

In Daniel we see the antichrist introduced as the "little horn," that comes out of the ten horns, or ten kingdoms of the end times.

> 7*After this I saw in the night visions, and behold, a fourth beast, dreadful and terrible, exceedingly strong. It had huge iron teeth; it was devouring, breaking in pieces, and trampling the residue with its feet. It was different from all the beasts that were before it, and it had ten horns.*
>
> 8*I was considering the horns, and there was **another horn, a little one**, coming up among them, before whom three of the first horns were plucked out by the roots. And there, in this horn, are eyes like the eyes of a man, and a mouth speaking pompous words.*
>
> Daniel 7:7-8 (emphasis added)

We don't have to try to interpret these verses, since someone who saw the vision with Daniel, probably an angel, gives the interpretation.

> *23...The fourth beast shall be a fourth kingdom on earth, which shall be different from all other kingdoms, and shall devour the whole earth, trample it and break it in pieces.*
> *24The ten horns are ten kings who shall arise from this kingdom. And* **another shall rise after them; he shall be different from the first ones, and shall subdue three kings.**
> *25He shall speak pompous words against the Most High, shall persecute the saints of the Most High, and shall intend to change times and law. Then the saints shall be given into his hand for a time and times and half a time.*
>   Daniel 7:23-25 (emphasis added)

Agreeing with Daniel 7:21, Daniel Chapter 8 narrows down the focus of who the little horn could be:

> *8Therefore the male goat grew very great; but when he became strong, the large horn was broken, and in place of it four notable ones came up toward the four winds of heaven.*
> *9**And out of one of them came a little horn**, which grew exceedingly great toward the south, toward the east, and toward the Glorious Land.*
>   Daniel 8:8-9 (emphasis added)

We are grateful to the Angel Gabriel, who interpreted the vision for Daniel.

> *21And the male goat is the kingdom of Greece. The large horn that is between its eyes is the first king.*
> *22As for the broken horn and the four that stood up in its place, four kingdoms shall arise out of that nation, but not with its power.*

*23And **in the latter time of their kingdom, when the transgressors have reached their fullness, a king shall arise**, having fierce features, who understands sinister schemes.*

24His power shall be mighty, but not by his own power; He shall destroy fearfully, and shall prosper and thrive; He shall destroy the mighty, and also the holy people.

Daniel 8:21-24 (emphasis added)

Thus, we see that the little horn, the antichrist, must arise out of one of the four divisions of Alexander's Greek empire.

A careful rendering of ancient Greek history shows that the "first king," Alexander the Great, died in 323 B.C. At that time, his kingdom was divided between four generals. They are the four kingdoms referred to in Daniel 8:22.

General		Geographical Area
General Cassander	took	Greece
General Lysimachus	took	Turkey
General Seleucus	took	Syria & Iraq
General Ptolemy	took	Egypt

Chart #3

The next verse, Daniel 8:23, makes it clear that the antichrist will arise from one of these four kingdoms. It's important to note that all four generals were Greek by nationality, as stated in Daniel 8:21. (Remember the antichrist must be of Greek national origin to satisfy Revelation 13:2. It is helpful to remember that the ancient Philistines migrated to Israel from the Aegean Islands, which are a part of

Greece. The modern name for Philistines is Palestinians. This could possibly explain the "Greek connection" of the antichrist.)

Antichrist is also called the "Assyrian" and the "King of Babylon." So let us take a closer look at General Seleucus, who ruled out of Antioch, Syria. Assyria included Syria, Lebanon, part of Turkey, Iran and Iraq; the borders were very fluid. Babylon conquered Assyria in 612 B.C. The combination of Babylon and Assyria is known as the "Fertile Crescent."

It is believed by many that the "Fertile Crescent" will be the power base of the future antichrist. Political events that are causing such havoc in the Middle East because of the Iraqi War make it seem plausible that Iraq and Syria may form some type of alliance. If that happens it would cause an Assyrian to also become the "King of Babylon" in the near future. Another title given the antichrist in Daniel 11 is "King of the North."

It appears we are looking for a man of Greek nationality, whose citizenship is in Syria, and will be called the "King of the North," who will one day seize Jerusalem as his base, and set an idol in the holy place. Has there ever been such an evil person on the face of the earth? The answer is "yes," the Seleucid king, Antiochus IV Epiphanes. King Antiochus Epiphanes was a ruthless Greek ruler from Syria who was determined to totally subjugate Jewish culture. Greek language and customs were thrust upon the Jews; and worship of Zeus, the Greek god was mandated. Antiochus IV ruled from 175 B.C. to 164 B.C. Fierce resistance by the Jews, rallied by a great warrior named Judas Maccabee, characterized the last three years of his reign. Jewish scholars see the Jewish military victory over Antiochus Epiphanes in 164 B.C. as a fulfillment of this prophecy written three hundred years before the war.

> *13For I have bent Judah My bow, fitted the bow with Ephraim, and raised up your sons, O Zion, against your sons, O Greece, and made you like the sword of a mighty man.*
>
> Zechariah 9:13

However, David Baron states emphatically "the prophecy cannot be altogether restricted to the Maccabean struggle with the Syrian Greeks."[4] David Baron was born in Russia in 1855 and raised in the best Rabbinical schools of Europe. He found Jesus to be Messiah while studying the Old Testament. His prolific writings were addressed to Jews and Christians alike. He goes on to explain:

> "No; Zion and Greece, as has been well observed by another writer, are in this prophecy of Zechariah opposed to one another as the city of God and the city of the world (the civitas Dei, and the civitas mundi," as Augustine has it), and the defeat of Antiochus Epiphanes and his successors at the hands of comparative handfuls of despised Jews, to which this passage may primarily refer, **foreshadows the final conflict with world-power, and the judgments to be inflicted on the confederated armies who shall be gathered against Jerusalem,** not only directly by the hand of God, but also by the hand of Israel, who shall then be made strong in Jehovah.[5] (emphasis added)

Thus we see the defeat of Antiochus Epiphanes by Judas Maccabee prefigures the defeat of antichrist by the Lord Jesus Christ.

The following comparisons between Antiochus Epiphanes and the coming antichrist include many chilling facts:

	ANTIOCHUS	ANTICHRIST
1. Called the "little horn."	Daniel 8:9	Daniel 7:8
2a. Outlaws the solemn feasts.	2 Maccabees 6:6	-------------
2b. Attempts to outlaw the feasts.	--------------------	Daniel 7:25
3. Takes away daily sacrifice.	Daniel 8:11	Daniel 9:27
4. Defiles the temple of God.	2 Maccabees 6:1	Daniel 9:27
5a. Compels the people to worship the god Bacchus or be put to death.	2 Maccabees 6:7-9	-------------
5b. Compels the people to worship the beast, his image, or take his number or be put to death.	--------------------	Revelation 13:15-17
6. Jews will suffer under his reign but not be forsaken by God.	2 Maccabees 6:16	Daniel 2:44 Daniel 7:25-26
7. Sets up the abominable idol of desolation on the altar of God.	1 Maccabees 1:57	Mark 13:14
8. Called the "King of the North."	Daniel 11:6	Daniel 11:40
9. Attacks & defeats Egypt.	Daniel 11:11-15	Daniel 11:40
10. An extended peace follows his overthrow.	Peace from 163 B.C. to 63 B.C. (100 years)	Revelation 20:5 (Jesus reigns for 1,000 years)

Chart #4

One of the notable differences between Antiochus Epiphanes and the antichrist has to do with religious beliefs. Antiochus Epiphanes was a pagan, while the antichrist will worship a *"god of forces"* (Daniel 11:38). Islam has always conquered by military force. Many modern scholars believe antichrist will be a Moslem military leader.

The Shiite Moslem doctrine of the "imamate" teaches that the twelfth prophet (descendant of Mohammad) disappeared in the desert in the 800's. He is allegedly a "sinless and absolutely infallible" holy man who will come back from the desert at the end of the age and lead the world into a totally Moslem society.[6] It is interesting to note that the Shiite branch of the Islamic faith is on the rise, particularly among the young and impoverished in Moslem countries. Mohammad's command to his followers before his death was: "Fight until all declare, there is no god but Allah."

Could that command be the driving force behind the war of terror that is currently being waged against us?

Before we leave the antichrist model, let us refer the reader back to #7 above. We will examine the term "abomination of desolation" in light of the Book of Maccabees. (Maccabees are considered historical, but not part of Scripture, except by the Catholic Church.)

Daniel warns of the abomination of desolation:

> *11And from the time that the daily sacrifice is taken away, and the abomination of desolation is set up, there shall be one thousand two hundred and ninety days.*
>
> Daniel 12:11

Jesus affirms the accuracy of Daniel's prophecy in Mark 13:14: *So when you see the 'abomination of desolation,' spoken of by Daniel the prophet, standing where it ought not"* — (let the reader understand) — *"then let those who are in Judea flee to the mountains.* And so we ask the question, what is the *"abomination of desolation?"* In the light of the Book of Maccabees, we understand that they are referring to an idol called in the Book of Revelation the *"image of the beast."* King Antiochus set up as an idol, a statue of Jupiter on the altar:

> *57On the fifteenth day of the month Casleu, the hundred and forty-fifth year, king Antiochus set up the abominable idol of desolation upon the altar of God.*
>
> I Maccabees 1: 57

We know from the Word of God that the false prophet will set up an image of the beast.

> *14And he deceives those who dwell on the earth by those signs which he was granted to do in the sight of the beast, telling those who dwell on the earth to make an image to the beast who was wounded by the sword and lived.*
> *15He was granted power to give breath to the image of the beast, that the image of the beast should both speak and* **cause as many as would not worship the image of the beast to be killed**.
>
> Revelation 13:14-15 (emphasis added)

In conclusion let us re-examine two important facts: 1) The Moslems are waiting for a world leader to come out of the desert and take over the world. 2) Half way through the Tribulation Period, (Daniel 9:27), antichrist will set up the image of the beast inside the Temple Holy Place. Consider the warning of Jesus to those who will be alive during the Tribulation Period, in light of these two facts:

> *25See, I have told you beforehand.*
> *26Therefore if they say to you, 'Look, **He is in the desert!**' do not go out; or 'Look, **He is in the inner rooms!**' Do not believe it.*
> Matthew 24:25-26 (emphasis added)

It is quite possible that the Lord is referring in this scripture to the Moslem world leader, *"He is in the desert,"* and the image of the beast, *"He is in the inner rooms."*

As we stated in Chapter 2 of this book, the Judgment of the Nations has already begun. What is the one thing holding back the four horsemen of the Apocalypse? The books have not been opened.

> *10b"The judgment was set, And the books were opened."*
> Daniel 7:10b (OKJ)

When the books are opened, the four horsemen will be released. But who will open the books?

Chapter 4

The Four Horsemen Defined

The entire 5th Chapter of the Book of Revelation is the story of who will open the book. (Although the new King James Version calls it a scroll, that is incorrect. "Scroll" is a correct translation of Revelation 6:14, but not a correct translation of the book in Revelation Chapter 5. Strong's call the "book" biblion, the diminutive of biblios, from which we get the word Bible.) A frantic search is made in heaven, then on earth, and finally, even in hell to find someone who is worthy to open the book. (Revelation 5:3) No one is found. John feels so helpless, he weeps much (Revelation 5:4). Why would John weep? Because he sees the Judgment of the Nations has begun. He knows the book must be opened, in order to conclude the time of judgment. After the judgment, the Messiah will come, and John's beloved country, Israel, will be returned to its rightful place. It will be the center of all earthly business, the ruling kingdom of the world. The Temple will be rebuilt, and there will be heaven on earth. Like any good Jew, he longs for this day.

What Joy! What Ecstasy!

Suddenly, standing before him, is "the Lamb that was slain." What joy! What ecstasy! Worship and praise follow. And then Jesus walks up to His Father, takes the book, and begins to break the seals. Thus, the book is opened.

Revelation Chapter 6 reveals that when the first four seals of the book are broken by Jesus, riders come riding on horses: white, red, black and green. The King James Version of the Bible refers to the fourth horse as the pale horse. However, the actual word in Greek translates as green. Much speculation has gone forth throughout the ages on this topic. Who are those riders, where are they going, and for what purpose? As stated in the Prologue of this book, *"It is also written in your law that the testimony of two men is true"* John 8:17. Surely, if we search the scriptures, we will find the four horses somewhere else besides the Book of Revelation. Knowing that the three great pieces of the "end times puzzle" are the books of Daniel, Zechariah and Revelation, we expect to find four horsemen in one of those books, and we are not disappointed.

Indeed, in Zechariah we find four horses in Chapter 1, and four chariots in Chapter 6. The book of Zechariah was written soon after the Jews returned to Israel from the seventy-year exile in Babylon, a punishment God had sent because of their disobedience and idol worship. Zechariah Chapters 1 through 6 contain a series of eight visions the prophet had in one night, which portray a "connected picture of the future of Israel linked on to the then existing time, and closing with the prospect of the ultimate completion of the Kingdom of God."[7]

Let us now consider the four horses of Zechariah Chapter 1:

> *8I saw by night, and behold, a man riding on a red horse, and it stood among the myrtle trees in the hollow; and behind him were horses: red, sorrel, and white.*
>
> *9Then I said, 'My lord, what are these?' So the angel who talked with me said to me, 'I will show you what they are.'*
>
> *10And the man who stood among the myrtle trees*

> *answered and said, 'These are the ones whom the Lord has sent to walk to and fro throughout the earth.'*
>
> *11So they answered the Angel of the Lord, who stood among the myrtle trees, and said, 'We have walked to and fro throughout the earth, and behold, all the earth is resting quietly.'*
>
> *12Then the Angel of the Lord answered and said, 'O Lord of hosts, how long will You not have mercy on Jerusalem and on the cities of Judah, against which You were angry these seventy years?'*
>
> Zechariah 1:8-12

In our judgment, these horses **could not** be the horses of the Apocalypse for several reasons:

1) There are two red horses, and Revelation Chapter 6 has only one red horse.
2) The man riding on a red horse in verse 8 is identified in verse 11 as the Angel of the Lord. "He is 'the Angel of Jehovah, who is none other than the 'Angel of His face,' the Divine 'Angel of the Covenant,' the second person in the Blessed Trinity."[8] Jesus could not be riding one of the horses, since He is in heaven breaking the seals.
3) Verse 12 puts the time of this vision as immediately following the Babylonian exile, approximately 520 B.C. The four horsemen will not go forth until the end of the age, probably very soon.

As we have indicated, the eight visions are sequential, as to time, and the eighth vision occurs right before dawn. Therefore, the vision of the four chariots, the final vision, would appear to fit chronologically during these end times. **The four chariots appear to be our introduction to the four horsemen.**

Let us now examine the vision of the four chariots of Zechariah: Chapter 6.

> *1Then I turned and raised my eyes and looked, and behold, four chariots were coming from between two mountains, and the mountains were mountains of bronze.*
>
> *2With the first chariot were red horses, with the second chariot black horses,*
>
> *3with the third chariot white horses, and with the fourth chariot dappled horses-strong steeds.*
>
> *4Then I answered and said to the angel who talked with me, 'What are these, my lord?'*
>
> *5And the angel answered and said to me, "These are four spirits of heaven, who go out from their station before the Lord of all the earth."*
>
> *6"The one with the black horses is going to the north country, the white are going after them, and the dappled are going toward the south country."*
>
> *7Then the strong steeds went out, eager to go, that they might walk to and fro throughout the earth. And He said, 'Go, walk to and fro throughout the earth.' So they walked to and fro throughout the earth.*
>
> *8And He called to me, and spoke to me, saying, 'See, those who go toward the north country have given rest to My Spirit in the north country.'*
>
> Zechariah 6:1-8

Much debate has centered around the words of verse seven, namely who are the "strong steeds?" Since the black, white and dappled horses are enumerated in verse six, we agree with the Septuagint Version of the Old Testament, which holds the "strong steeds" of verse seven to be the red ones.

Furthermore, we agree with David Baron's translation of verse 8 to be correct, as we note that "ruach," translated in the King James as "Spirit" can also be translated "anger." Thus the eighth verse should read instead as: *"See, those who go to the north country have caused my anger to rest on the north county."* (Zechariah 6:8) "The meaning of the 8th verse, then, is that that company of invisible host whose mission was toward the north country caused God's anger to rest on it."[9] Therefore, when we compare the chariots of Zechariah Chapter 6 with the mission of the horsemen in Revelation Chapter 6, we will see the events, which have caused God's anger to rest on the north country.

And so, as we have just indicated, we believe the four horses of Revelation Chapter 6 are indeed another look at the four chariots of Zechariah Chapter 6. We hold this view for several reasons:

1) The horses of Zechariah's chariots are: red, black, white and dappled (i.e. spotted).
2) The horses of the Apocalypse are: red, black, white and green. [pale in KJV] (The mystery of why the "dappled" horses, which we identify as Rome, are classified as green in the New Testament will be discussed in a later chapter).
3) Chronologically, the four horsemen come on the scene at the beginning of the Tribulation Period. The Lord's return is then depicted seven years later in the Book of Revelation.

In the book of Zechariah, the four chariots are introduced in Zechariah 6:1-8.

Notice that the return of the Lord comes soon after their assignment is completed four verses later:

> *12...From His place He shall branch out, And He shall build the temple of the Lord;*
> *13Yes, He shall build the temple of the Lord. He shall bear the glory, And shall sit and rule on His throne; So He shall be a priest on His throne, And the counsel of peace shall be between them both.*
> Zechariah 6:12-13

4) The four chariots are identified for us in Zechariah 6:5. They are "the four spirits of heaven, who go out from their station before the Lord of all the earth."

In order for our analogy to be accurate, the four horses of the Apocalypse must be good, i.e. "spirits of heaven." A careful reading of the text in Revelation, Chapter 6 indicates that **it is the riders who**

cause such calamity to come upon the earth. The horses are God's agents who facilitate the judgments that are to come upon the earth.

> *1Now I saw when the Lamb opened one of the seals; and I heard one of the four living creatures, saying with a voice like thunder, 'Come and see.'*
>
> *2And I looked, and behold, a white horse. And he* ***who sat on it had a bow****; and a crown was given to him, and he went out conquering and to conquer.*
>
> *3When He opened the second seal, I heard the second living creature saying, 'Come and see.'*
>
> *4Another horse, fiery red, went out, And* ***it was granted to the one who sat on it to take peace from the earth****, and that people should kill one another; and there was given to him a great sword.*
>
> *5When He opened the third seal, I heard the third living creature say, 'Come and see.' And I looked, and behold, a black horse, and* ***he who sat on it had a pair of scales*** *in his hand.*
>
> *6And I heard a voice in the midst of the four living creatures saying, 'A quart of wheat for a denarious, and three quarts of barley for a denarious; and do not harm the oil and the wine.'*
>
> *7When He opened the fourth seal, I heard the voice of the fourth living creature saying 'Come ands see.'*
>
> *8And I looked, and behold, a pale horse.* ***And the name of him who sat on it was Death****, and Hades followed with him. And power was given to them over a fourth of the earth, to kill with sword, with hunger, with death, and by the beasts of the earth.*
>
> Revelation 6:1-8 (emphasis added)

Therefore, we believe the four horses are the same "four spirits of heaven" that go forth in the book of Zechariah. Notice that they are sent out by the four living creatures, also called the four "Cherubs" in the book of Ezekiel. With voices like thunder they give the command to "come and see," and the horses are released.

The four living creatures, whose assignment is to "send out" the horses, represent the four earthly directions upon which judgment must come. The world is described in the Bible as a giant cosmic house, complete with a cornerstone.

> 4Where were you when I laid the foundations of the earth? Tell Me, if you have understanding,
> 5who determined its measurements, surely you know! Or who stretched the line upon it?
> 6To what were its foundations fastened? Or who laid its cornerstone?
>
> Job 38:4-6

When the sixth seal is opened, cosmic disturbances shake the earth.

> 12I looked when He opened the sixth seal, and behold, there was a great earthquake and the sun became black as sackcloth of hair, and the moon became like blood.
> 13And the stars of heaven fell to the earth, as a fig tree drops its late figs when it is shaken by a mighty wind.
> 14Then the sky receded as a scroll when it is rolled up, and every mountain and island was moved out of its place.
>
> Revelation 6:12-14

Thus, we see a picture of judgment going throughout the earth, **but in a limited way**, during the time of the Wrath of the Lamb. A careful reading of the Book of Revelation indicates that there are two different three and a half year periods during the Tribulation. The first half is called the "Wrath of the Lamb," Revelation 6:16, and the second half, the "Wrath of God," Revelation 14:7. (See Chart #1) For our purpose in this chapter, it is important to see the assignment of the four horsemen is to bring judgment to the part of the earth that surrounds the Mediterranean Sea: Europe, the Middle East, Northern Africa, and also to Russia.

5) Finally, the matching of the four chariots of Zechariah with the four horsemen of Revelation, including the direction and purpose of their mission, works together "hand in glove." Zechariah tells us who they are and where they are going. Revelation tells us why.

So who are they? Again, we trust David Baron to explain:

"The number four clearly brings to our mind again the four great Gentile world-powers whose successive course makes up "the times of the Gentiles," and whose final over-throw must precede the restoration and blessing of Israel, and the visible establishment of the Messianic Kingdom." [10]

"These four are the Babylonian, the Medo-Persian, the Grecian (or Graeco-Macedonian), and the Roman. "These are the horns (or Gentile powers) which have scattered Judah, Israel, and Jerusalem" (chap. I. 19), and it is the overthrow and judgment of these, by means of invisible heavenly powers appointed of God as a necessary precursor to the establishment of Messiah's kingdom, and the blessing of Israel, which is symbolically set forth to the prophet in this last vision." [11]

And so, the mystery is revealed. The first time the chariots are introduced is in Zechariah 6:2-3. They are in chronological order here. We take their identity from these verses.

Then in Zechariah 6:6-7 we see which direction they are going. This helps us greatly when we come to Revelation. For in Revelation Chapter 6 we have their missions explained.

Identity and Purpose of the Four Chariots/Horsemen

	Color	Country	Mission	Direction	Order of Appearance (In Revelation)
1st Chariot	RED	Babylon (Iraq)	Take a sword (Islam) throughout the earth	To the whole earth	Second
2nd Chariot	BLACK	Medo-Persia (Iran)	Famine and hunger in Iran, Russia and all the countries that fought Israel in the Ezekiel war	North	Third
3rd Chariot	WHITE	Greece	The antichrist leaves Israel after the Peace Treaty of Dan. 9:27 and goes north to coalesce his base.	North	First
4th Chariot	DAPPLED /GREEN	Rome	Given power over ¼ of the earth (The early Roman empire also dominated ¼ of the earth) The evil twins, "Death and Hell," kill with war, hunger, beasts of the earth and their own evil spiritual power.	South	Fourth

Chart #5

The mission of each horseman will be examined more closely in Chapter 7. The conclusions we draw are based on a combination of:

1) What the scriptures say
2) What Bible teachers have taught
3) Current events
4) Our own interpretations

Thus, we readily admit that one could easily differ with our opinion. We invite the reader to study the scriptures and come up with other probable scenarios. Our purpose is to stir in the heart of the reader, a sense of imminence, regarding the events about which we write.

Chapter 5

A Dappled/Green Horse

As we have stated, the four world powers that are subject to judgment, according to Zechariah and Revelation are:

1) Babylon (Iraq) .... Red Horse
2) Medo-Persia (Iran) .... Black Horse
3) Greece .... White Horse
4) Rome .... Dappled/Green Horse

Chart #6

These are the ancient enemies and oppressors of God's chosen people.

In the Book of Daniel, these same four empires are first illustrated prophetically in Chapter 2, in Nebuchadnezzar's image.

1)	Babylon	Head of gold	Daniel 2:32
2)	Medo-Persia	Chest and arms of silver	Daniel 2:32
3)	Greece	Belly and thighs of bronze	Daniel 2:32
4)	Rome	Legs of iron	Daniel 2:33
5)	Revived Rome	Feet of iron and clay	Daniel 2:41-43

Chart #7

Of the feet of iron and clay Daniel says:

> *41Whereas you saw the feet and toes, partly of potter's **clay and partly of iron**, the kingdom shall be divided; yet the strength of the iron shall be in it, just as you saw the iron mixed with ceramic clay.*
> *42And as the toes of the feet were partly of iron and **partly of clay**, so the kingdom shall be partly strong and partly fragile.*
> *43As you saw **iron mixed with ceramic clay**, they will mingle with the seed of men; but they will not adhere to one another, just as iron does not mix with clay.*
> Daniel 2:41-43 (emphasis added)

Daniel repeats three times the vision of iron mixed with clay. It is possible the feet of the image had a spotted or "dappled" appearance. More than a hundred years later, when Zechariah wrote his book and called the horses of the fourth chariot "dappled," there must have been much curiosity about who this fourth and final kingdom would be. Clearly, from the prophets, the Jews could conclude it would be a strong and cruel empire.

Despised And Pagan Rome

By the time John wrote the book of Revelation on the island of Patmos, all Jews knew who the fourth kingdom was, because they were much oppressed by it. This fourth kingdom was Rome – their conqueror, their subjugator

– despised and pagan Rome.

John personally had much to fear from Rome. They had tried to boil him in oil, but he didn't die. So the emperor Domitian had him exiled to the island of Patmos.

Let us consider again the four chariots of Zechariah versus the four horses of the Apocalypse.

Kingdom	Zechariah's Chariots	John's Horses
Babylon	Red	Red
Medo-Persia	Black	Black
Greece	White	White
Rome	Dappled	Green

Chart #8

Why does the color not match in the Roman horse? We believe that John knew, as did all the Jewish Christians of his era that Zechariah and Daniel had prophesied severe judgment would befall the fourth kingdom, according to Scripture. **John could not risk his own life and the lives of fellow believers by linking Rome with the books of Zechariah and Daniel.** Therefore, we believe, either John or the Lord encoded Rome in a color that would not fit the pattern: chloros, in Greek, or green. (The King James incorrectly identifies the horse as pale. However, the word chloros is used to describe "green grass" in Revelation 8:7 and "neither any green thing" in Revelation 9:4. We get our word "chlorophyll" from this word.)

We observe that John also employed this same vehicle, encoding the name for Rome, in Revelation 17. We identify Rome in Revelation 17:9 as a city that sits on seven hills. Also, in Revelation 17:18 Rome is identified as "the great city that reigns over the kings of the earth." As previously discussed in this chapter, the "ten toes" of Daniel, Chapter 2, are the kings who reign in the revived Roman Empire. A careful reading of the 17th Chapter of Revelation reveals that John calls that city, which is actually Rome, "Mystery Babylon the Great" in verse five, and "the harlot" in verses 15 and 16. Again, we feel this was encoded to prevent the ire of the Romans from falling on the Jewish Christians.

The color of the Roman horse, green, will still have significance, of course. Never, in the entire Bible, is a word ever wasted or without meaning. Could it be that the green represents a radical left wing movement that is currently sweeping Europe? We are referring to the environmental movement, which hold that "Mother Earth" is sacred - namely, Greenpeace or the Green Party.

Chapter 6

World Conflict/World Harvest

When General Titus, the Roman warrior, surrounded and sacked Jerusalem in 70 A.D., the Jews were enslaved and taken to the four corners of the earth. It is a testament to God's faithfulness that they were never assimilated into the culture of any nation to which they were assigned. God had called the Jews to be a holy nation:

> 5Now therefore, if you will indeed obey My voice and keep My covenant, then you shall be a special treasure to Me above all people, for all the earth is Mine.
> 6And you shall be to Me a kingdom of priests and a holy nation. These are the words which you shall speak to the children of Israel.
>
> Exodus 19:5-6

The Jews were required to depart from the promised land three times:

1) During the famine in Jacob's day when they went to Egypt, where they were fed by their brother Joseph, whom God had sent ahead to

preserve them.
2) In 586 B.C. when King Nebuchadnezzar took them to Babylon for seventy years.
3) In 70 A.D. when Titus the Roman dispersed them throughout the world.

God had always promised them that their ultimate end would be to return to Israel, the center of the earth, to rule and reign with Him forever.

> *14Also the sons of those who afflicted you shall come bowing to you, all those who despised you shall fall prostrate at the soles of your feet; And* **they shall call you The City of the Lord, Zion of the Holy One of Israel.**
> *15Whereas you have been forsaken and hated, that no one went through you, I will make you an eternal excellence, joy of many generations.*
> Isaiah 60:14-15 (emphasis added)

> *2And behold, the glory of the God of Israel came from the way of the east. His voice was like the sound of many waters; and the earth shone with His glory.*
>
> *5The Spirit lifted me up and brought me into the inner court; and behold, the glory of the Lord filled the temple.*
> *6Then I heard Him speaking to me from the temple, while a man stood beside me.*
> *7And He said to me, 'Son of man, this is the place of My throne and the place of the soles of My feet,* **where I will dwell in the midst of the children of Israel forever...'**
> Ezekiel 43:2; 5-7 (emphasis added)

The nation of Israel was reborn on May 15, 1948. When the United Nations agreed to give the Jews their land back because they had suffered so in the holocaust, literal hell broke loose. Because Jesus Himself will rule and reign from Jerusalem, the devil has refused to allow the Jews to live in peace.

The wars the Jews have endured since May 15, 1948 include:

1) 1948 – the war for independence
2) The 1956 War
3) 1967 – the Six Day War
4) 1973 – the Yom Kippur War
5) 2000 – the Intifada

The Intifada, or War of Terror, is ongoing as we write this book. The term "suicide bomber," or more accurately "homicide bomber," is a vehicle used by Satan to destroy Jews and Arabs. Only God knows how many young Moslems have descended into hell for eternity, awakened to the stark reality that it was not God who encouraged them to commit murder.

The Bible clearly teaches that the devil will once again try to wrest the Holy Land from the grasp of the chosen people. A certain war, called the war of Gog and Magog, or the war of Ezekiel 38 and 39, even now is on the radar screen, as we look at current events.

Every country has been assigned a special angel to protect it by God. Likewise, Satan has assigned to each country a "chief prince," to destroy it. The chief prince over Russia is a sinister being named "Gog." While no unanimity exists among Bible scholars as to who Gomer and Togarmah are, in general, the players in the Ezekiel War line up as the following:

Biblical Name	Modern Name
Rosh	Russia
Meshech	Moscow (Western capital of Russia)
Tubal	Tobulsk (Eastern capital of Russia)
Persia	Iran
Ethiopia	Ethiopia
Libya	Libya
Gomer	Germany
Togarmah	Turkey
Gog	The evil spirit ruling Russia

Chart #9

The hordes of Gog, listed above will come against the tiny country of Israel to plunder and destroy it. What are the events that will precipitate this massive war? As stated in Chapter 2, we believe Syria will invade Israel. Israel will counterattack, leveling Damascus. In the natural, it will be the Israeli destruction of Damascus that causes Russia and her allies to invade Israel. In the spiritual realm, it is God who ordains the attack.

Notice in the **God Ordains The Attack** following verses depicting the Ezekiel War, where the Lord God Himself is speaking, commanding the nations to invade Israel:

> *7Prepare yourself and be ready, you **and all your companies** that are gathered about you; and be a guard for them.*
>
> *8After many days you will be visited. In the latter years **you will come into the land** of those brought back from the sword and gathered from many people on the mountains of Israel, which had long been desolate; they were brought out of the nations, and now all of them dwell safely.*
>
> *9**You will ascend**, coming like a storm, covering the land like a cloud, **you and all your troops** and many peoples with you.*
>
> *10**Thus says the Lord God**: "On that day it shall come to pass that thoughts will arise in your mind, and **you will make an evil plan**:*
>
> *11You will say, 'I will go up against a land of unwalled villages; I will go to a peaceful people who dwell safely, all of them dwelling without walls, and having neither bars nor gates'—*
>
> *12'to take plunder and to take booty, **to stretch out your hand** against the waste places that are again inhabited, and against a people gathered from the nations, who have acquired livestock and goods, who dwell in the midst of the land.'*
>
> Ezekiel 38:7-12 (emphasis added)

The purpose of the war, from the adversary's point of view, is to take plunder and take booty, and to come against Israel, according to verse 12.

The nations of the world, including the United States, will lodge a diplomatic protest, but not interfere militarily:

> 13Sheba, Dedan, the merchants of Tarshish, and all their young lions will say to you, 'Have you come to take plunder? Have you gathered your army to take booty, to carry away silver and gold, to take away livestock and goods, to take great plunder?'
>
> Ezekiel 38:13

Many Christian scholars consider Americans to be the "young lions of Tarshish." Tarshish is seen by various authors to be the northern Mediterranean area, Spain or England. Since the pilgrims were of European descent, any of the above definitions of Tarshish would qualify Americans to be their offspring, or young lions.

Against all odds, the Jews will win the war. To be more precise, the great God, Jehovah, will win the war. He has many weapons at His disposal. They include:

1) Earthquake: "Surely in that day there shall be a great earthquake in the land of Israel." Ezekiel 38:19b
2) Military Might: "I will call for a sword against Gog in all My mountains..." Ezekiel 38:21a
3) Friendly Fire: "...Every man's sword will be against his brother." Ezekiel 38:21b
4) Pestilence and Bloodshed: "And I will bring him to judgment with pestilence and bloodshed..." Ezekiel 38:22
5) Rain, Hail, Fire and Brimstone: "I will rain down

on him, on his troops, and on the many peoples who are with him, flooding rain, great hailstones, fire and brimstone." Ezekiel 38:22

It is our view that the war of Ezekiel 38 and 39 will precede the Tribulation Period. (See Chart #10). The Church will have her finest hour, as God uses us to bring in the great harvest for which we have prepared so long.

Thus, we will present the evidence, which we feel places the Ezekiel War before the Tribulation Period: (See following chart)

Event	Ezekiel War	Armageddon
Where it will be fought	Mountains of Israel Ezek. 38:21; 39:2	Valley of Armageddon Joel 3:14; Rev. 16:16
When it will be fought (see chart page 4)	6th Day, "Latter Days" Ezek. 38:8; 16	7th Day, "Day of the Lord" Zech. 14:1; Joel 2:1; Obad. verse 15; Rev. 1:10
Concluded by	Treaty of Dan. 9:27	Jesus defeating the Nations. Zech. 14:3; Rev. 19:11-21
Nations participating	Russia, Iran, Ethiopia, Libya, Germany, Turkey Ezek. 38:3, 5, 6	All Nations Zech. 12:3; Zech. 14:2; Obad. verse 15
Position of Jerusalem when war begins	At peace Ezek. 38:11	"Trampled down." Luke 21:24b; Daniel 9:6
Position of Israelis when war begins	At peace Ezek. 38:14	Hiding in Petra Rev. 12:13-16; Isa. 16:1-4; Dan. 11:41
Purpose of the war	Bring in the harvest Ezek. 38:16b, 23; Ezek. 39:7b, 21	Set up the millennial reign with Israel presiding Isa. 42:4; Zech. 14:16-21 Rev. 20:4

Chart #10

As we have indicated above, the Lord God Himself orders the invasion and then destroys the invaders. God, who is love, ordered the invasion. But, we might ask, why would He do that?

1) God is just, and must bring judgment on those who come against His chosen people.

> *19"For in My jealousy and in the fire of My wrath I have spoken..."*
>
> Ezekiel 38:19

2) God is merciful and this war will trigger the great world harvest.

> *16b"**...so that the nations may know Me**, when I am hallowed in you, O Gog, before their eyes."*
>
> Ezekiel 38:16b (emphasis added)

> *23"Thus I will magnify Myself and sanctify Myself, and **I will be known in the eyes of many nations**. Then they shall know that I am the Lord."*
>
> Ezekiel 38:23 (emphasis added)

> *7"So I will make My holy name known in the midst of My people Israel, and I will not let them profane my name anymore. Then **the nations shall know that I am the Lord**, the Holy One in Israel."*
>
> Ezekiel 39:7 (emphasis added)

> *21"I will set My glory among the nations; **all the nations shall see My judgment** which I have executed, and My hand which I have laid on them.*
>
> Ezekiel 39:21 (emphasis added)}

3) Israel will finally, as a nation, turn back to Jehovah, (however, they will not recognize their Messiah yet).

> *22So the house of Israel shall know that **I am the Lord** their God from that day forward.*
>
> Ezekiel 39:22 (emphasis added)

Let us pause here to reflect on the lifestyle of the modern man and woman. Most of us watch television for two to four hours a day. Since the Vietnam conflict, we have become accustomed to watching war on television.

In the Iraqi War in 2003, we even had reporters "embedded" with the troops, so we could watch the war unfold, "play by play." How many hours a day did we watch television during the war? Thus it has become a part of our national psyche to see war "live and in color" on our television set.

An Arab/Russian Alliance Formed To Teach Israel A Lesson

Use your own imagination and project yourself into the days of the Ezekiel War. We are alarmed to see Russian troops moving into position! An alliance, much like our coalition against Iraq, will probably coalesce. Nations will decide to "teach Israel a lesson," once and for all. It has to happen, because God spoke it through Ezekiel.

Television newsmen will be bringing us updates, minute by minute. Christians will, no doubt, be holding prayer meetings around the clock: *"Father, let your will be done on earth as it is in heaven."* Nominal Christians and fence sitters will dust off the Word and check it out_Ezekiel 38 & 39.

Suddenly, the attack! Paratroopers descend on the mountains of Israel, *"covering the land like a cloud,"* _ Ezekiel 38:9 _ *"all your troops and many peoples"* against a country of five million Jews. (Flashback to Gideon, who defeated innumerable Midianites with three hundred men.) Could it really be? Could the Bible be true?

And then, earthquake, sword, fire and brimstone, hail and rain. God reigns, He really is in control. _ Oh praise Him forever more!

Nations Come To The Lord!

Nations, yes nations, will come to the Lord. This will be the great harvest, for which we have waited so long. We will reap where we have not sown, the plowman will overtake the reaper, the former and the latter rain together. The knowledge of the glory of the Lord will cover the land as the water covers the seas, and we will be right in the middle of it all.

Christians open their Bibles to Ezekiel 38 and read fast and furious. Someone knocks at your door, the phone rings, the same question from every neighbor, every friend, "You're a Christian aren't you? What's happening?" Saints of God, learn it now, so you will be prepared. We must respond rightly. We will tell them, "This is only the beginning. God is judging the nations. Repent, and be saved. Accept Jesus and escape the wrath to come."

> 34But take heed to yourselves, lest your hearts be weighed down with carousing, drunkenness, and cares of this life, so that Day come on you unexpectantly.
> 35For it will come as a snare on all those who dwell on the face of the whole earth.
> 36Watch therefore, and pray always **that you may be counted worthy to escape all these things that will come to pass**, and to stand before the Son of Man.
> Luke 21:34-36 (emphasis added)

> 9**For God did not appoint us to wrath**, but to obtain salvation through our Lord Jesus Christ,
> 10who died for us that whether we wake or sleep, we should live together with Him.
> I Thessalonians 5:9-10 (emphasis added)

> 10"Because you have kept My command to persevere, **I also will keep you from the hour of trial which shall come upon the whole world**, to test those who dwell on the earth.
> 11Behold, I am coming quickly! Hold fast what you have, that no one may take your crown."
> Revelation 3:10-11 (emphasis added)

Dear saints of God, we are being called by the Holy Spirit in this hour to prepare. Now is the time to begin, if you have not already heard His command: longer seasons of prayer every day, taking communion, regular seasons of fasting, joining a cell group, studying and meditating in the Word, enrolling in that Bible Study offered by your church, using your vacation to attend a good Christian seminar, etc. In short, it's time to set your heart on course, so you will be found *"without spot or wrinkle."*

Some will not accept the mantle, however. Sadly, they will miss the rapture. It will be their lot to see a middle level Syrian diplomat travel to Israel, to negotiate a peace treaty with the victorious and ebullient Israelis. It is our view, that his offer will include allowing the Jews to rebuild the temple on Mount Moriah. They have been yearning for a temple since 70 A.D., and it's too good a deal to turn down. Why will a Syrian be the negotiator? It may be that Syria will be the presiding nation at the United Nations Security Council, (they presently are presiding, as we write this book). Another possible reason is because the war was precipitated by the Syrian invasion of Israel. In any event, the Bible is clear, he is the antichrist, coming to the Israelis with a seven-year peace treaty:

> *27Then he shall confirm a covenant with many for one week; but in the middle of the week he shall bring an end to sacrifice and offering. And, on the wing of abominations shall be one who makes desolate, even until the consummation, which is determined, is poured out on the desolate.*
> Daniel 9:27

As we review Daniel 7:10 and 11 we notice that the first thing Daniel heard when the books were opened was the sound of the antichrist's voice.

> *10b...The judgment was set, and the books were opened.*
> *11aI beheld then because of the voice of the great words* **which the horn spake...**
> Daniel 7:10b, 11a (OKJ Emphasis added)

Why was the antichrist's voice the first thing Daniel heard when Jesus opened the seals? The first four seals in Revelation Chapter 6 release the four horsemen of the Apocalypse. Does the first seal release the antichrist?

Read on to see if the Book of Revelation agrees with what we have just read here in the Book of Daniel.

Chapter 7

The Four Horsemen Explained

Part I - The Rider on the White Horse

| 3rd Chariot | On the White Horse | Represents Greece | The antichrist leaves Israel after the Peace Treaty of Dan. 9:27 and goes north to coalesce his base. | Goes North | First to appear in Revelation |

Chart #11

1Now I saw when the Lamb opened one of the seals; and I heard one of the four living creatures say with a voice like thunder, "Come and see."
2And I looked, and behold, a white horse. And he who sat on it had a bow; and a crown was given to him, and he went out conquering and to conquer.
Revelation 6:1-2

The earth is in chaos and confusion, due to the millions (and, we pray, even billions) of saints who have disappeared in the rapture. Perhaps the most powerful man on earth, the President of the United States, will be among the missing. America has been the conscience of the world. As peace-keeper, chastiser of rogue nations and provider of food, aid and medicine to the poor, she has had no equal. In the revival that accompanies the Ezekiel War, most Americans have recommitted their lives to the Lord Jesus. Therefore, it is possible that two hundred million Americans depart in the rapture. (This is our fervent prayer.)

The world needs leadership. They turn for help to the brilliant diplomat who did what no one else could do _ brought peace to the Middle East. This man, antichrist, is given a bow, military power, and a crown, legal authority, to assume power in the Arab World. Going north from Jerusalem, he unites the following Arab nations, which are in chaos for the reasons listed:

Syria – devastated by the leveling of Damascus.
Iraq – still not stable after the Gulf War of 2003.
Iran and Turkey – These countries (as well as Russia, Germany, Libya and Ethiopia) have lost 84 percent of their young men in the Ezekiel War. Never, in modern warfare, has there been such devastation.

> *1"Behold, I am against thee, Oh Gog, the prince of Rosh, Meshech and Tubal,*
> ***2And I will turn thee back, and leave but a sixth part of thee."***
> Ezekiel 39:1-2 OKJ (emphasis added)

Lebanon – a poor vassal state of Syria, has been pulled down economically with Syria.

Therefore, we see the antichrist, an Islamic military leader, going north from Israel to create an alliance of these countries: Lebanon, Syria, Iran, Iraq and Turkey. In ancient times these countries had often been one big confederation known as the "Fertile Crescent." All pagan religions found their genesis in the Fertile Crescent where many deities were worshipped. Abraham was called out of the Fertile Crescent, to separate himself unto God.

We believe that the antichrist will rule out of the Fertile Crescent for the first three and a half years of the Tribulation Period. He will probably spend much time at the headquarters of the European Union, which is presently in Brussels, Belgium.

He will also have a "home base" out of which to operate. In ancient times, the leading cities of the Fertile Crescent were Ninevah and Babylon. Babylon will be the center of economic power during the Tribulation Period according to Zechariah 5:5-11 and Revelation Chapter 18. It is worthy to note that kings of Assyria, Babylon, Persia and Greece all had palaces in the ancient city of Babylon. Alexander the Great, who conquered the known world, died in Babylon. The Bible clearly relates the antichrist to these four countries. He is referred to in Scripture as:

The Assyrian – Micah 5:5-6
The King of Babylon – Isaiah 14:4
He has feet like a bear (Persian implied) – Revelation 13:2
Son of Greece – Zechariah 9:13

We therefore conclude that the rider on the white horse, the antichrist, conquers the Arab world first, and sets up his headquarters in Babylon.

Part II - The Rider on the Red Horse

Before we embark on an explanation of the rider on the red horse, it is important to understand the history of monotheistic religion. Monotheistic religion is the belief in only one God. There are only three monotheistic religions: Judaism, Christianity, and Islam. All three of these religions hold Abraham to be their father. All three of these religions believe a ruler will rise up from their religion at the end of days to rule the world. Amazingly, all three are correct, setting up the climax of human history.

<u>Jewish doctrine states:</u>
I believe, with complete faith that Messiah will come.

<u>Christianity doctrine states:</u>

God will send Jesus, Whom heaven must receive until the time of the restoration of all things. (Acts 3:21)

Moslem doctrine states:
Fight until all declare there is no God but Allah. And Muhammad is his prophet

Furthermore, the Moslems are waiting for an Islamic prophet to come out of the desert at the end of days to lead the entire world into the Islamic faith. (See Chapter 3, second paragraph after Chart # 2)

One author opines that the three crosses on Calvary represent the three monotheistic religions. Jesus Christ took the place of all Christians when He took the death sentence, which we deserved. The good thief represents the Jew, condemned to death by the law, but acknowledging his Messiah just in time. Sadly, the other thief represents Moslems, who continue to reject the one true God until they descend into perdition![12]

It is our opinion that Jews, Christians, and Moslems will all see their heroes on the center stage of world history very soon. First, the antichrist will appear, the rider on the white horse. He will be a Moslem military leader. Seven years later, the Jews will see Messiah, as He sets His feet on the Mount of Olives. No surprise to those who converted to Christianity after the rapture, the Jewish Messiah is none other than our own Lord and Savior, Jesus Christ.

Let us now consider the rider on the red horse.

1st Chariot	On the Red Horse	Represents Babylon (Iraq)	Take a sword (Islam) throughout the earth	Goes to the whole earth	Second to appear in Revelation

Chart #12

3When He opened the second seal, I heard the second living creature saying, "Come and see."

> 4Another horse, fiery red, went out. And it was granted to the one who sat on it to take peace from the earth, and that people should kill one another; and there was given to him a great sword.
>
> Revelation 6:3 & 4

It is interesting to note that the rider on the red horse is the only horseman given permission to go throughout the whole earth. Approximately 1.25 billion of the 6 billion people living today are Moslem. Mosques are springing up in traditionally Christian countries at an alarmingly rapid rate.

Martyrdom of infidels – those who do not accept Allah, and Mohammad as his prophet – has historically been an acceptable way to spread Islam. Thus, we are not surprised to see that the rider on the red horse is given a "great sword." We believe the "great sword" represents Islam and the Moslem fundamentalists who spread their faith by the sword. Decapitation has long been a method of execution in Eastern cultures. The Philistines beheaded King Saul (I Samuel 31:9) and Herod had John the Baptist beheaded (Matthew 14:8). In recent history, Daniel Pearl, a Jewish New York <u>Times</u> reporter, was beheaded by the Pakistanis in 2002. Therefore, we are not surprised to learn that martyrdom by decapitation will be used against followers of Jesus during the Tribulation Period:

> 4And I saw thrones, and they sat on them, and judgment was committed to them. And I saw the **souls of those who had been beheaded** for their witness to Jesus and for the word of God, who had not worshipped the beast or his image, and had not received his mark on their forehead or on their hands. And they lived and reigned with Christ for a thousand years.
>
> Revelation 20:4 (emphasis added)

The world had expected the antichrist to usher in an era of peace and security. He was the architect of the brilliant peace plan after the Ezekiel War (see third paragraph after Chart #10). Instead, he gives his Islamic followers permission to go throughout the world, spreading the Moslem ideology by the sword. Therefore, there will be no peace. The great apostle Paul had forewarned them:

> *2For you yourselves know perfectly that the day of the Lord so comes as a thief in the night.*
> *3For when they say,* **"Peace and safety then sudden destruction comes upon them***, as labor pains upon a pregnant woman. And they shall not escape.*
> I Thessalonians 5:2, 3 (emphasis added)

The rider on the white horse, the antichrist, goes north. The rider on the red horse goes to the whole world. Next, we will consider the rider on the black horse, who also travels north.

Part III - The rider on the Black Horse

| 2nd Chariot | On the Black Horse | Represents Medo-Persia (Iran) | Famine and hunger in Iran, Russia and all the countries that fought Israel in the Ezekiel war | Goes North | Third to appear in Revelation |

Chart #13

We see in Zechariah 6:6 that the rider on the black horse actually **precedes** the antichrist (the rider on the white horse) into the north country.

> *6"The one with the black horses is going to the north country, the white are going after them, and the dappled are going toward the south country."*
> Zechariah 6:6

In other words, famine and devastation are already causing severe problems in Iran before Jesus opens the seals. The Ancient Medo-Persian empire included Iran, Iraq, Turkey and Southern Russia.

The devastation had already begun during the Ezekiel War (see Chart #1). Iran and the other combatants had suffered a casualty rate of a staggering 84 percent of their troops in that war.

> *1Therefore, thou son of man, prophesy against Gog, and say, Thus saith the Lord God, Behold, I am against thee, O Gog, the chief prince of Meshech and Tubal:*
> *2And I will turn thee back, and leave but **the sixth part of thee**, and will cause thee to come up from the north parts, and will bring thee upon the mountains of Israel:*
> Ezekiel 39:1 - 2 (OKJ Emphasis added)

> *Such high casualty rates had occurred in Old Testament times. (Numbers 31:7; Joshua 6:21; I Kings 11:15 - 16; II Kings 19:35)*

But never, in a modern military confrontation, had a nation lost 5/6 of its soldiers. God seems to have punished not only the military, but also the homelands of these armies. (Ezekiel 38:2 indicates that "Magog" refers to Russia).

> *6"And I will send fire on Magog and on those who live in security in the coastlands. Then they shall know that I am the Lord."*
> Ezekiel 39:6

Let us consider the rider on the black horse according to the translation of Zechariah 6:8 provided for us by David Baron (see page 44).

> *6...See those who go to the north country have caused my anger to rest on the north country.*

In the spirit realm, the Ezekiel War had been precipitated by the bonding together of two very powerful and very evil spirits: Islam and Communism. God's anger had rested on the countries whose leaders embraced these spirits. Thus, these countries had reaped judgment: Iran, Syria, Turkey, Russia and possibly Germany. All of the above, the north country, have been bastions of anti-Semitism for generations. They have persecuted God's Chosen People, the apple of His eye. Beginning during the Ezekiel War, and progressing through the tribulation period, they will be reaping all the evil they have sown.

John sees that the rider on the black horse, who was sent to the north country, has a pair of scales in his hand. The only direct quotation John hears, during the episode with the four horsemen, is spoken when the black horse is released. John hears a voice speaking from heaven. Let us consider what the voice says:

> 6*And I heard a voice in the midst of the four living creatures saying, "A quart of wheat for a denarius; and three quarts of barley for a denarius: and do not harm the oil and the wine."*
>
> Revelation 6:6

In John's day a denarius was one day's wages for a laborer. This quote seems to imply that an entire day's pay will be needed to buy mere staple foods to subsist on. In fact, this kind of severe poverty already exists in some third world countries.

Severe Poverty And Excessive Luxury

Some Biblical scholars believe the words *"and do not harm the oil and wine"* indicate that a few, probably the leadership of these countries, will live in excessive luxury while their people suffer. We saw a clear picture of that scenario in Saddam Hussein's Iraq.

Thus, we have a dismal scene in the countries north of Israel. Scarcity of food, starvation which causes disease to flourish, inconsolable grief at the loss of so much life, and a shortage of manpower due to the deaths of the military. Conditions are ripe for this Hitler-like antihero, who rides to the north country. The people will no doubt be eager to hear his diabolical plan to make them powerful and wealthy again!

Part IV - The Rider on the Green Horse

4th Chariot	On the Dappled\Green	Represents Rome	Given power over ¼ of the earth. The evil twins, "Death and Hell," kill with war, hunger, beasts of the earth and their own evil spiritual power.	Goes South	Fourth to appear in Revelation

Chart #15

Before we discuss the riders associated with the fourth and final horse, we must clarify who they are. Their names are Death and Hell, and they appear together throughout the Bible.

To understand Death and Hell, we must first comprehend this truth:

In the Bible the same name is often given to people and to a geographic location.

Thus, we will see that Death and Hell are evil spirits, and also a place where spirits go.

We will look at several examples, to help solidify this concept in our thinking:

Name	Represents People/Spirits	Represents Geographical Location
Jerusalem	Matt.23:37 "O Jerusalem, Jerusalem…I wanted to gather your children together"	John 5:1 "Jesus went up to Jerusalem"
Israel	Matt. 2:6b "Who will shepherd My people Israel?"	Matt. 2:20a "…go into the land of Israel…"
Bride of Christ	Rev. 19:7 "…the marriage of the Lamb has come, and His wife has made herself ready."	Rev. 21:9b, 10 "Come, I will show you the bride, the Lamb's wife…and (he) showed me the great city…"
Death and Hell	Rev. 6:8 "…the name of him who sat on it was Death and Hades followed with Him…"	Rev. 20:13a "…Death and Hades delivered up the dead who were in them.

Chart #16

Death and Hell are seen throughout the Bible, working together. Their purpose is always to destroy men's souls. We presume that Death encourages human beings to continue in sin until it kills them (Romans 6:21, 23). Then Hell scoops them up at the moment of death and carries them off to hell. Let us consider some of the nefarious deeds of Death and Hell:

1) They incited the demented King Saul to try to destroy David.
    6The sorrows of Sheol surround me; the snares of death confronted me.
    II Samuel 22:6

2) They persuaded the rulers of Jerusalem to look to Egypt instead of Jehovah for protection.
    14Therefore hear the word of the Lord, you scornful men, who rule the people who are in Jerusalem.
    15Because you have said, "We have made a covenant with death, and with Sheol we are in agreement.
    Isaiah 28:14, 15

3) The Babylonians covenanted with Death and Hell. Death and Hell assisted them in destroying Jerusalem in 586 B.C.:
    5Because he enlarges his desire as hell, and he

is like death, and cannot be satisfied, he gathers to himself all nations and heaps up for himself all peoples.

Habakkuk 2:5

4) The apostle Paul quotes the final victory over them in I Corinthians 15:55:

55"O Death, where is your sting? O Hades, where is your victory?"

5) Jesus Himself refers to them as a place:

18"I am He who lives, and was dead, and behold, I am alive forevermore, Amen., And I have the keys of Hades and of Death."

Revelation 1:18

As we read Revelation 6:8, we notice that only Death sits on the green horse. Hell, or Hades, follows with him. We will now investigate their assignment, as the judgment of planet earth continues.

7When He opened the fourth seal, I heard the voice of the fourth living creature saying, "Come and see."
8So I looked, and behold, a pale (green) horse. And the name of him who sat on it was Death, and Hades followed with him. And power was given to them over a fourth of the earth, to kill with sword, with hunger, with death, and by the beasts of the earth.

Revelation 6:7, 8 (parenthesis added)

At the beginning of the tribulation period, the revived Roman Empire will probably approximate the borders of the European Union. The Europeans have a mindset foreign to independent-minded American thinking. They want to give up their national identity. They have been gradually assimilating into one group for over fifty years for this goal — they want to be the most powerful political and economic bloc in the world!

The European Economic Community was founded in 1952 with

a document called the "Treaty of Rome." It is our view that the desire to give up national identity to revive an ancient political entity is being driven by evil spirits. Could those evil spirits be Death and Hell?

According to Revelation 6:7 these spirits have the power to kill with the sword. We see this sword as military and political power. It is interesting to note that the United Nations transferred the task of policing Bosnia to the European Union on January 1, 2003.[13] Furthermore, in May of 2003, the European Union ordered "180 Airbus A400 military transport jumbo jets with the capacity to deploy up to 20,000 troops."[14] As we write this book, a mighty military machine is being assembled within the European Union.

How will Death and Hell, the spirits we believe are ruling the European Union, *"kill with hunger"* in Revelation 6:7? To understand this political maneuver, it is necessary to understand genetically engineered food.

Genetically engineered food, pioneered in the United States, is food that has been scientifically altered to resist disease and insects without excessive pesticides. Often, it is also engineered to be more nutritious. Approximately 60 to 70 percent of America's exported grain is genetically engineered.[15]

As part of its radical, left wing environmental policy, the European Union objects to these foods. They are blocking the export of genetically engineered foods from the United States, through the United Nations, to third world countries. Thus we see that Death and Hell are already killing with hunger.

The prophet Daniel described the revived Roman Empire with two separate analogies (see Chapter 3 Chart #2 and Chapter 5 first two pages) As the ten toes of Nebuchadnezzar's image, it looked like this:

> *40And the fourth kingdom shall be as strong as iron, inasmuch as iron breaks in pieces and shatters everything; and like iron that crushes, that kingdom will break in pieces and crush all the others.*
>
> Daniel 2:40

As the fourth great beast in Daniel, Chapter 7, he saw it like this:

> *19Then I wished to know the truth about the fourth beast, which was different from all the others, exceedingly dreadful, with its teeth of iron and its nails of bronze, which devoured, broke in pieces, and trampled the residue with its feet;*
>
> *20and the ten horns that were on its head, and the other horn which came up, before which three fell, namely, that horn which had eyes and a mouth which spoke pompous words, whose appearance was greater than his fellows.*
>
> Daniel 7:19 - 20

Notice that in the image of the great beast its teeth are iron, representing Rome.

According to the Book of Revelation, the first direction the green horseman goes is south. Remember that the end time struggles are primarily a spiritual battle for wealth and power!

After the rapture, the earth will be in chaos, with one to two billion people raptured. America will be greatly weakened, since two thirds of her population went to heaven. (This is our fervent prayer.) The antichrist went north, as we have already seen. The Europeans, the dominant world power since the rapture, see antichrist's power rising. To counter his fame, Rome turns south to woo Egypt and the rest of Africa. They'd better grab what power they can, to maintain their primacy! Egypt, Libya and Ethiopia ally themselves with Rome, completing the Revival of the ancient Roman Empire. (It is our view that the three kings the antichrist attacks and defeats mid tribulation are three of Rome's Islamic allies: Egypt, Libya and Ethopia. Let the readers study Daniel 11:40, 42, 43 in many translations to understand this concept.)

We conclude this book with the release of the four horsemen, the beginning of the seven-year period known as the time of Jacob's trouble. The reader is encouraged to continue on, reading what John, the beloved apostle, was so diligent to record.

The Promise Of A Blessing

The Book of Revelation is the only book in the Bible that begins and ends with the promise of a blessing to those who read it. In Revelation 1:3, John is the one who offers us a blessing. In Revelation 22:7, it is our Lord Himself who promises us we will be blessed if we read Revelation. Dare we ignore the word He Himself has spoken, knowing that the time is at hand!

Epilogue

As Jesus releases the four horsemen of the apocalypse, the judgments known as the seven seals and the seven trumpets commence. The first three and a half years of the tribulation are called *"the Wrath of the Lamb"* in Revelation 6:16. The Wrath of the Lamb concludes mid-tribulation, when antichrist seizes Jerusalem (Daniel 11:45; Revelation 11:7). At that appointed time *"the Wrath of God"* is initiated, as described in Revelation 14:7 (see Chart #1).

And so in the middle of the tribulation, as referenced in the prologue, the Mystery of God will be finished. We believe the words *"there should be time no longer"* refers to the end of the Church age:

> 6And sware by him that liveth for ever and ever, who created heaven, and the things that therein are, and the earth, and the things that therein are, and the sea, and the things which are therein, **that there should be time no longer:**
> 7But in the days of the voice of the seventh angel, when he shall begin to sound, **the mystery of God should be finished**, as he hath declared to his servants the prophets.
> Revelation 10:6-7 OKJ (emphasis added)

The Mystery of God includes the assignment of the Church to

preach to the principalities and powers in the heavens:

> *9and to make all see what is the fellowship of the mystery, which from the beginning of the ages has been hidden in God who created all things through Jesus Christ;*
> *10to the intent that now* ***the manifold wisdom of God might be made known by the church to the principalities and powers in the heavenly places.***
> Ephesians 3:9-10 (emphasis added)

The seventh trumpet, also called the third woe, has toppled Satan and his minions from the heavenlies. Thus, that preaching assignment of the Church has concluded:

> *7And war broke out in heaven: Michael and his angels fought with the dragon; and the dragon and his angels fought,*
> *8but they did not prevail, not was a place found for them in heaven any longer.*
> *9So the great dragon was cast out, that serpent of old, called the Devil and Satan, who deceives the whole world;* ***he was cast to the earth, and his angels were cast out with him.***
>
> *12"Therefore rejoice, O heavens, and you who dwell in them!* ***Woe*** *to the inhabitants of the earth and the sea!* ***For the devil has come down to you,*** *having great wrath, because he knows he has a short time."*
> Revelation 12:7-9, 12 (emphasis added)

And so, like falling dominoes, the mid-tribulation events include:

1) The end of the Wrath of the Lamb
2) The end of the Church Age
3) The casting of Satan and his forces to earth.

4) The judgment of the saints in heaven. (Revelation 11:18)
5) The flight of the Jews from Israel to Petra for three and a half years (Revelation 12:6 & 14)
6) The initiation of the Wrath of Jehovah, which begins with an open heaven:

> *17Saying, We give thee thanks, O Lord God Almighty, which art, and wast, and art to come; because thou hast taken to thee thy great power and hast reigned.*
> *18And the nations were angry,* ***and thy wrath is come****, and the time of the dead, that they should be judged, and that thou shouldest give reward unto thy servants the prophets, and to the saints, and them that fear thy name, small and great;* ***and shouldest destroy them which destroy the earth.***
> *19...****And the temple of God was opened in heaven****, and there was seen in his temple the ark of his testament...*
> Revelation 11:17-19a OKJ (emphasis added)

(It is interesting to note that the wrath of the Lamb also began with an open heaven in Revelation 6:16)

The revelation of Jesus is so rich and exciting we urge the reader to continue on. In its essence, this book is not to teach you what will shortly come to pass. We see through a glass darkly like everyone else. From the Hidden is primarily a vehicle to drive the reader back to the Bible, where the precious Holy Spirit will be the instructor.

For the reader whose interest has been piqued, we are preparing a second work on the soon coming end of the age. We are heartened by a passage written by the great prophet, Jeremiah, 2500 years ago, to our generation:

You Will Understand It Perfectly

18For who has stood in the counsel of the Lord, And has perceived and heard His word? Who has marked this word and heard it?

19Behold, a whirlwind of the Lord has gone forth in fury—A violent whirlwind! It will fall violently upon the head of the wicked.

20The anger of the Lord will not turn back until He has executed and performed the thoughts of His heart. ***In the latter days you will understand it perfectly.***

Jeremiah 23:17-20 (emphasis added)

A Word From The Author

Has something in this book frightened you?

Turn back to Page 63 of Chapter six and read the scripture from Luke Chapter 21, I Thessalonians Chapter 5 and Revelation Chapter 3. It is clear from these scriptures that the Church of Jesus Christ will escape the wrath to come. Refer also to the chart, *Judgment of the Nations,* which illustrates an event called the "the Rapture of the Church." The Church will be taken into heaven and Jesus wants you to be one of those who escape. (The Rapture of the Church will be explained in detail in book two, <u>Understanding the End of the Age</u>.) Being a member of the Church of Jesus Christ is not a matter of what denomination you belong to, or where you go to church. To be a member of His Church, or His Body, is determined by the intent of your heart, which only God can see. If you are unsure of your status with God, say this prayer with genuine conviction:

Heavenly Father, I know I am a sinner. Though I've fallen short of Your glory so many times, I truly believe that Jesus died on the cross so that I <u>(state your name)</u> could have eternal salvation.

Jesus, I thank you for dying on the cross for me, I invite you now to come into my heart, take over my life, show me Your will for my life. I promise that from this day forward, I will live for You and follow Your will for my life. Fill me with Your Holy Spirit and empower me to do Your will. Amen.

If you said this prayer, please write the author and she will send you a copy of the Gospel of John and a few suggestions on how to get started in your new life as a child of God. She can be reached at:

Theresa Garcia
Box 494
Columbia, Il 62236
Phone: 1-877-860-4900; Pin #548-168
Or: 1-618-281-3291
www.fromthehidden.com
Email: docandt@htc.net

Endnotes

[1] Jeffrey Satinover, M.D., Cracking the Bible Code, Harper Collins Publishers, Inc., New York, New York, pages 273 and 275, 1998
[2] Kenneth Copeland, Living at the End of Time—A Time of Supernatural Increase. Kenneth Copeland Publications, pages 20, 21, 22, 1997, 1998
[3] Billye Brim, "The Glory Watch," page 13, Spring 2002, A Glorious Church Fellowship, Branson, Missouri
[4] David Baron, Zechariah, A commentary on His Visions and Prophecies, reprint, Kregel Publications, Grand Rapids, Michigan 1956, page 327
[5] Ibid, page 327
[6] Belleville News Democrat, "Divisions in Islam rooted in actions of followers after death of Mohammed," Sunday, March 23, 2003, page 7A, Belleville, Illinois
[7] Op cit Baron, page 22
[8] Ibid Baron, page 23, emphasis added
[9] Ibid pages 182, 183
[10] Ibid page 176
[11] Ibid, page 179
[12] Gwen Reeser, Your Carriage Is Waiting, Creation House Press, page 125, 2001
[13] Belleville News Democrat, "EU takes over policing of area," page 5A, January 2, 2003, Belleville, Illinois
[14] News Max.com Wires, www.newsmax.com/archives/articles/2003/5/27
[15] Senator Bill Frist, interviewed by Tony Snow, "Fox News Sunday with Tony Snow," Sunday, May 25, 2003